EYE
THE OFFICIAL GAMEBOOK

EYE
THE OFFICIAL
GAMEBOOK

Ian Bailey

Devised and produced by Hatch. Written and edited by
Ian Bailey

Virgin

Published by
the Paperback Division of
W.H. ALLEN & Co Plc

A Virgin Book
Published in 1987
by the Paperback Division of
W. H. Allen & Co Plc
44 Hill Street
London W1X 8LB

Copyright © 1987 by Ian Bailey

Printed in Great Britain by
Anchor Brendon Ltd, Tiptree, Essex

ISBN 0 86369 256 7

To Sebastian,
who passed on whilst this book
was in preparation

Ian Bailey studied English and Anglo-Saxon at the University of York. On graduating he joined the Games Industry and has since worked in Britain, America and Sweden. He spent several years as the Head Buyer, and finally a director, of a UK games company. In 1985, after the publication of two books and a board game he gave up his job to co-found Hatch, a design and consultancy group. He recently founded Hatch Games Limited, which will be releasing a range of products based on the works of James Clavell.

CONTENTS

INTRODUCTION

Eye is a strategy game which is simple to play but not so easy to master. Its rules are straightforward; the complexity and challenge lie in the ingenious design of its board and the interaction between the different colours and players. As a result Eye is suitable for anyone, be they a casual player or a games buff. When you first play, luck will rule the game but as you learn more about Eye it will become a true battle of skill between the players.

I first saw the game when one of its inventors, Billy Barry, brought a prototype to me. I found the board's ability to move and the kaleidoscope of colours fascinating – playing on four different game boards at the same time, which is the effective result of the Eye board's ability to change, was a novel challenge.

I must confess I found Eye infuriating at first, because it was so easy to lose the game by making just one wrong turn of the wheels. I began studying the different patterns the board created and the relationship between them, and as I did so I began uncovering more and more information and the games we were playing became far more challenging.

This book contains all the information you will need to master the strategy of Eye. It is not presented as a definitive study but rather as a handbook which will increase your awareness of the game and its tactics and in so doing raise your chances of winning.

I would like to use this opportunity to express my special thanks to Martin Colbourne, the chief designer of Eye, who had to play a lot of games with me to develop the tactics revealed in this book.

1. HOW IS EYE PLAYED?

Before you embark on the following chapters it is important you have a copy of Eye for reference and a full understanding of the rules. The rules included with the game are adequate but brief and I have therefore included an expanded set here, which should clear up any doubts you may have.

Eye is a strategy game for one to four players. It is played on a unique rotating board, which presents four different playing surfaces, over which the players compete. The object of the game is to capture your colour.

The Board

Eye's board consists of a coloured base covered by two plastic spiral wheels. The wheels can be rotated either independently or together in a clockwise or anti-clockwise direction. By turning the wheels you will alter the colour pattern of the playing surface.

As you rotate the wheels you will discover four different playing surfaces or patterns. The patterns are named after the shapes they form: Short Spirals, Straight Lines, Long Spirals and Circles.

The wheels cover 75 per cent of the board's base. As a result only 32 of the 128 squares are visible at any one time. The squares are coloured with eight hues: Red, Blue, Yellow, Green, Pink, Grey, Orange and Mauve. Four squares of each colour appear in each of the patterns.

The Playing Pieces

There are two types of token in Eye.

The barrel-shaped tokens are the playing pieces. There are eight of these playing pieces for each of the player colours: Red, Blue, Yellow and Green. Two of these pieces are spares and have been included in case you lose some of the tokens.

The flat counters are called 'Markers'. There is one marker for each of the eight colours in the game. Markers are used by players to record which board colours they have captured during the course of play.

Preparing For Play

Each player selects a colour. In the two-player game the colours used must be Red and Blue. They then draw a number of their colour's playing pieces according to the table below:

Game Version	Number of Playing Pieces
Two Players	Six each
Three Players	Four each
Four Players	Three each

The players decide who will go first. If there is any argument the owner of the game should go first. The player to the right of the player who is going first then decides which pattern the board will begin the game on. The first player then places one piece on the board in any one of the coloured squares. The other players follow suit, with play passing round the table in a clockwise direction. This process continues until all the pieces have been placed on the board. Players should note that only one playing piece can ever occupy a square. You are now ready to play the game.

Movement

The number of movement points a player has is calculated at the beginning of each of his turns. It depends on the largest number of pieces he has on the same colour at that time.

For Example:

It is the Blue player's turn. He has three pieces on Red

squares, two on Green squares and one on a Yellow square. Because he has three pieces on the same colour (in this case Red) he has three moves. Only the largest number is ever used and a player must take all of his moves.

There are two types of movement in Eye. A player may turn the wheels or move his pieces in any combination up to the limit of his movement points.

It costs one movement point to move one playing piece of your colour (you can only move your opponent's pieces by turning the wheels) from its square to any adjacent unoccupied square. You cannot move into or through a square occupied by another piece. The diagrams below show which squares are deemed to be adjacent for the purposes of the game.

DIAGRAM I: EXAMPLES OF MOVEMENT
TO ADJACENT SQUARES

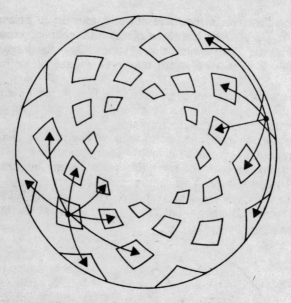

**DIAGRAM 2: EXAMPLES OF MOVEMENT
TO ADJACENT SQUARES**

It costs one movement point to move one wheel one step.
A step is the width of one spiral arm. Each wheel can be
moved in either direction.

Winning Eye

The victory conditions of Eye vary according to the
number of players who start the game.

Two Players: The winner is the first player to occupy
                all four of his colour squares on any one
                pattern.

Three Players: In the three-player game, if you capture another player's colour that player is knocked out of the game. As a result there are two ways of winning:

The winner is either the first player to occupy at least three of his colour's squares on any one pattern whilst the fourth square is free of any other player's token.

Or the last player to be left in the game.

Four Players: In the four-player game if you capture another player's colour that player is knocked out of the game. As a result there are two ways of winning:

The winner is either the first player to occupy at least two of his colour's squares on any one pattern, whilst the other two squares are free of any other player's token.

Or the last player to be left in the game.

Players should note you can only capture a colour during your turn. You can never capture a colour during another player's turn.

Capturing Other Colours
During the course of play players can capture colours other than their own. Such a move may eliminate another player in the three- and four-player versions of the game, but generally it will only increase your control of the board.

To capture a colour other than your own you must occupy its squares according to the same conditions as those required to win by capturing your own colour. For instance, in a three-player game you must occupy at least

13

three of the colour's squares on any one pattern whilst the fourth square is free of any other player's token.

You may capture a colour at any time during your turn. You cannot claim the capture of a colour in another player's turn, even if in turning the wheels, he moves your pieces into a capture position.

When you capture a colour other than your own, take its marker and place it in your 'indicator zone'. You will find this zone on the inside of the game box cover.

The Benefits Of Capturing Colours

In the three- and four-player versions of Eye if you capture another player's colour you knock him out of the game.

When you capture a colour you retain control of it for the rest of the game. At the beginning of all your subsequent turns, before you move, you may remove any other player's pieces which are on the colour you control. These pieces are moved to any other square on the board of your choice.

Once you have captured a colour it may not subsequently be taken away from you by another player, even if they fulfil all the requirements to make a capture. The only exception to this rule occurs in the two-player game, where your opponent may still capture his own colour, even if you control it.

Board Blocks

There are certain squares on the inner and outer edges of the board which if occupied will restrict the movement of the wheels. Care is needed when you move the wheels to ensure you sense these blocks and stop trying to turn the wheel. If you force the wheel the blocking pieces will pop out of the board. If a player moves a wheel and then finds it is blocked he does not lose his movement point but may then take another action instead.

Optional Rules For the Strategy Game
These options are included for use at your discretion and only with the agreement of all the players. Only one should be used at a time.

- Players can capture a colour controlled by another player. If they take such a colour they should remove its marker from the other player's indicator zone and place it in their own zone. All benefits of control pass to the new owner.
- The first player to capture an agreed number of colours wins the game.
- In the two-player version only, a player may win by capturing his or her opponent's colour.
- In the two-player game only, each player nominates three colours. The first player to capture any three of the colours so nominated wins the game.
- For a fast game that is ideal for younger players the first person to capture a colour wins the game.
- Handicapping – expert players should have to capture more colours to win the game than novices.

The Trivia Game
Each colour is given a category of questions. If there are insufficient categories then the surplus colours should be wild and any category may be chosen. A player's colour may never be designated a wild colour.

The object of the game is to capture your own colour or, in the three- and four-player versions, to be the last player left in the game.

The rules for the Trivia Game are the same as the Eye Strategy Game except:

At the start of the game, a piece can only be placed on the board if a question, corresponding to the colour the piece is to be placed on, is answered correctly. If it is answered incorrectly the piece is not placed and the next player takes his turn.

Players may move their pieces on the board before they have placed all of their tokens. However, if they choose to move instead of placing a piece they cannot use one of their movement points to place a piece.

Once on the board, if a piece is moved from one colour to another one on which the moving player has no other pieces, then a question belonging to the colour to be moved to must be answered correctly if the move is to succeed. If it is answered incorrectly the move fails and the player loses the movement point. No questions need be answered to move the wheels.

Special Two-Player Trivia Rules
Each player has four pieces only.

To capture a colour a player must occupy all four of its squares on any one pattern and then answer a question correctly of that colour's category. If the question is answered incorrectly the colour is not captured that turn.

Special Three-Player Trivia Rules
Players have four pieces only.

To capture a colour they must fulfil the same conditions as in the two-player trivia game.

A player is knocked out of the game if his colour is captured by another player.

Special Four-Player Trivia Rules
Players have three pieces only.

To capture a colour they must occupy three of its squares on any one pattern whilst the fourth is free of any other player's token, and then answer a question correctly of the appropriate category. If the question is answered incorrectly the colour is not captured that turn.

A player is knocked out of the game if his colour is captured by another player.

Solitaire Eye

Set the board on its Long Spiral pattern, with the Red Long Spiral in the position marked on the diagram below. Then place six playing pieces in the squares marked with a solid circle.

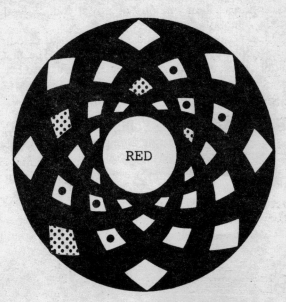

DIAGRAM 3: SOLITAIRE STARTING POSITION

The object of the solitaire game is to capture all eight colours.

Solitaire Movement

On the first turn you may move one piece one square or move one wheel one step.

17

Thereafter, a piece may only move if it starts from a colour at least one other piece is also occupying. The piece may only be moved to an adjacent square. Alternatively, you may move one wheel one step.

Capturing Colours In Solitaire Eye

To capture a colour you must occupy all four of its squares on any one pattern.

Once a colour has been captured the next colour must be captured on a different board pattern. The first four colours must all be captured on different patterns. The next four colours must be captured in the same sequence of patterns as the first four colours.

Winning And Losing Solitaire Eye

If you succeed in capturing all eight colours according to the requirements of the rules you have won.

If after any move all six of your pieces are on different colours the game is over and you have lost.

2. KNOW YOUR BOARD

The first thing to strike you on opening Eye is its colourful board. The second will be the realisation that the spiral wheels can be rotated to alter the colour pattern.

The ability to change the board pattern is unique to Eye. It is also the most important strategy element in the game. If you can understand and master the dynamics of the board you will be well on your way to winning your first game of Eye, through skill rather than luck.

This chapter explains how the board works, how to recognise the four patterns it produces and how to move between them in the shortest number of moves.

DIAGRAM 4: THE EYE BOARD WITHOUT THE
SPIRAL WHEELS

The Construction Of The Board

The board consists of three components. A coloured base and two counterpoised spiral wheels.

The base is a coloured pattern of 128 lozenges or in rule terms 'squares'. Diagram 4 shows you what the board looks like if the spiral wheels are removed.

The base is made up of eight colours, each of which fill sixteen of its squares. It is worth noting here that whilst the colours share an equal number of squares they are not distributed across the base in a symmetrical pattern. The asymmetrical pattern (see chapter three) is a deliberate design feature; it ensures each position of the spiral wheels will create an easily recognised colour pattern. It also means that each colour needs to be played in a slightly different way. This adds variety to the game but means that some colours are easier to play than others. The distribution of the colours and the balance between them is studied in chapter three, 'Know Your Colour'.

DIAGRAM 5: THE INNER WHEEL

DIAGRAM 6: THE OUTER WHEEL

The spiral wheels are fixed over the base and may be rotated in either a clockwise or anti-clockwise direction. The wheels have been designed to rotate independently of each other. It is well worth your while getting used to moving the wheels smoothly. You will find the inner wheel rotates freely. However, care is needed when turning the outer wheel. Do not place your fingers on top of the outer wheel but against its side as it moves more easily this way.

The arms of the wheels spiral out from the centre of the board in opposite directions. The inner wheel's arms spiral out in an anti-clockwise direction (diagram 5) whilst the outer wheel's arms spiral out in a clockwise direction (diagram 6).

The attitude of the wheel's spirals dictates how they move the playing pieces across the board. If you want to move the pieces out toward the edge of the board, you must turn the inner wheel clockwise or the outer wheel anti-clockwise. The reverse is true if you want to move the pieces into the centre of the board. To keep your pieces in the same position relative to the edges of the board but move them either one step to the left or right, turn both wheels simultaneously in the direction you require.

These elementary facts are well worth remembering. Different colours need to have their playing pieces in different areas of the board. For instance, to capture his Circle, Red needs his pieces in the centre of the board, whilst Green wants his pieces on the outer edge.

Place some pieces on the board and get used to how the wheels move them around. You will find that in some positions the pieces will stop you from moving one of the wheels in a particular direction. These positions are known as 'blocks' and they can be useful tools during the course of a game. The existence of the blocks means it is important you are moving the wheels smoothly, as otherwise you may not feel the block and in forcing the wheel the piece will pop out of the board. Of course, if you are feeling particularly nasty and you are losing a game you could use this effect to stop play! However, if you learn everything in this book you should not need to sink to such a level.

It is the opposition between the two wheels' arms that defines the playing surface. The wheels conceal 75 per cent of the base. As a result only 32 squares are ever on view at any one time. The eight colours fill four of those squares each.

As you move the wheels you will notice their arms form two basic shapes. These shapes are called the Open Eye (Diagram 7) and the Closed Eye (diagram 8).

DIAGRAM 7: THE OPEN EYE

DIAGRAM 8: THE CLOSED EYE

Even though there are only two shapes each one actually appears twice! The difference is one of about 15 degrees and it is enough to allow the wheels to form four different colour patterns. Take either one of the wheel shapes and study the colour pattern. Then move both wheels either one step clockwise, one step anti-clockwise or one step in opposite directions. You will discover the wheels are still in the original shape but the colour pattern has changed.

The Patterns

The four playing surfaces in Eye are named after the patterns they form. On the Open Eye you will find the Circle and Straight Line patterns. On the Closed Eye you will find the Long and Short Spirals. The form the four patterns take is shown below to help you recognise them.

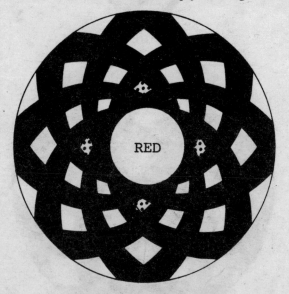

DIAGRAM 9: THE CIRCLE PATTERN

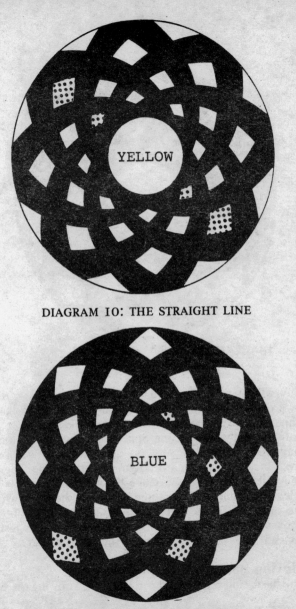

DIAGRAM 10: THE STRAIGHT LINE

DIAGRAM 11: THE LONG SPIRAL

DIAGRAM 12: THE SHORT SPIRAL

You will note a colour's name appears in the centre of each of the diagrams. This tells you the colour of shaded squares. If you position your Eye board so that the position of the Blue Long Spiral matches its position in diagram 11 you will be able to see where the other colours are. Once you have matched your board to one diagram you will find that as you move between the patterns the relevant colours will continue to match those shown on the other diagrams. This system is used throughout the book and you will find it especially useful when testing yourself against the problems in the final chapter.

Moving Between The Patterns

The basic skill required to win at Eye is knowing the four

patterns and the quickest way to move between them. When ever you play Eye never forget that you are not just playing on the pattern which is visible, you are playing on the three hidden ones as well. The skilled player will form his pieces into the shape of one of the hidden patterns whilst blocking the visible one, and then on his turn he will change the board and execute a winning move.

The following chart tells you how to move from any one pattern to another in the shortest number of wheel turns.

To use the Pattern Chart follow these instructions. Look at the pattern the board is on at present; then select the pattern you would like to move to and follow the movement instruction.

There are three movement instructions:

A: Move the inner wheel one step in either direction.
B: Move the outer wheel one step in either direction.
C: Move the inner and outer wheels one step each in the same or opposite directions.

Board Position	Desired Position	Wheel Movement
Short Spiral	Straight Line	B
	Long Spiral	C
	Circle	A
Straight Line	Short Spiral	B
	Long Spiral	A
	Circle	C
Long Spiral	Short Spiral	C
	Straight Line	A
	Circle	B
Circle	Short Spiral	A
	Straight Line	C
	Long Spiral	B

You should practise these moves until they are second nature. If you do not feel up to such an exercise then just make sure you have this chart to hand every time you play Eye.

How To Use Your Knowledge Of The Board

The board has been designed to produce four set patterns. Therefore, your first tactic should be to try and position your pieces so they assume the shape of one of the patterns. Such positioning means that when the board changes to your target pattern you will either capture a colour or win the game.

Unless you can capture a visible colour pattern in one turn you would be ill-advised to start building your pieces up into that pattern's shape. To move pieces toward a visible pattern without capturing it will invite the other players to retaliate. There are no rules in Eye for taking another player's piece, like there are in chess, so if they occupy just one square of the colour you are aiming for, your build up will have been wasted. In such a situation the only way to clear your colour of the opponent's piece is to move the wheels. However, this will change the pattern and your original build up will still have been in vain.

The clever player will build up for a pattern that is not yet visible using his knowledge of how the patterns relate and what shape they take. By building up your pieces into a pattern that is not yet visible you will attract less attention from the other players. You will be pleasantly surprised by the number of players who forget or simply do not know how the patterns relate. As a result they will either fail to block your build up or unwittingly move the wheels and change the board to the pattern you want. Many games are won or lost this way.

When building up for a hidden pattern always bear in mind how you are going to move the wheels to reach your target. If you build up on the wrong side of a wheel's spirals you will miss the colour you want.

There are certain general characteristics the patterns have which are important to remember.

The player colours (Red, Blue, Yellow and Green) on the Straight Line pattern are all on the inside of the board, so to win you must not end up on the edge. Therefore, it is important you bear in mind how the wheels move the pieces.

DIAGRAM 13: THE POSITION OF THE PLAYER COLOURS ON THE STRAIGHT LINE PATTERN

If you are aiming for the Long or Short Spirals always ensure you build up your formation so that it spirals out from the centre of the board in a clockwise direction. This is because the colours are printed on the board so they all spiral in a clockwise direction. If you accidently form an anti-clockwise spiral not only will you fail to capture anything but you will also have wasted all the turns it took to build the formation and those it will take to change it.

DIAGRAM 14: THE CORRECT WAY
TO BUILD UP FOR A SHORT SPIRAL

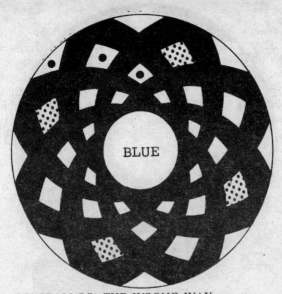

DIAGRAM 15: THE WRONG WAY
TO BUILD UP FOR A SHORT SPIRAL

Set up your board as it is shown in diagram 14 with blue
pieces in the positions marked. Then turn the inner wheel
one step anti-clockwise to see the result. Do the same
with diagram 15 to get an idea of the difference.

When it is not visible the Long Spiral is the hardest
pattern for players to relate to. The trick to remembering
this formation is as follows. Firstly, memorise where the
inner foot of your Long Spiral is. It will always be five
squares away (counting both hidden and visible squares)
in a clockwise direction from the inner foot of your
colour's Short Spiral. Once you have found the foot of
your Long Spiral, you will know its other squares are
spread over the next three spirals (always remembering
there will be one spiral in between each one) and each
one will be one square further out from the centre.
Diagram 16 shows this clearly.

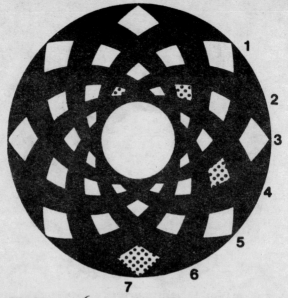

DIAGRAM 16: THE SHAPE OF THE LONG SPIRAL AND HOW IT IS SPREAD OVER THE BOARD

If you are aiming for your Circle pattern make sure you build up in the right area of the board. For instance, if Red builds up near the edge of the board he will not capture his colour because Red's Circle is on the inside of the board. The position of the different colours in each pattern is revealed in chapter three 'Know Your Colour'.

Experience and knowledge will ultimately tell you which are the best patterns for each colour to build up. As a general guide the hardest build ups for other players to detect are for the Long Spiral and Circle because these involve your pieces being spread out across the board. The concentration of pieces involved in a Short Spiral pattern or Straight Line makes them far easier to spot.

Your knowledge of the board can be used not only to

assist your capture of the various colours but also to thwart your opponents' build ups. Looking back to the pattern chart you will see each pattern has what can be called a weak relation. The weak relations are those patterns which are two instead of one wheel movement apart. The weak relations are:

Short Spiral to Long Spiral
Circle to Straight Line

When a player builds up his pieces into one of the Spiral patterns, moving the board to the opposite Spiral will weaken his position. It may also force him to break up his formation as he will have to act to protect the new pattern from capture by another player. This tactic works well with the Spirals because for each colour they are always in different areas of the board (see chapter three). It is more risky with the Circle and Straight Line patterns. This is because their squares are normally in the same areas of the board and your opponent will be able to switch between them with some ease.

When moving the wheels to weaken an opponent always turn them in the opposite direction to the way in which your opponent wants to move. It is recommended you practice these defensive moves so they become second nature. To do this place three or four pieces of one colour on the board so they are all occupying their own colour's squares. Then turn a wheel so they are one pattern away from winning. Now start moving the wheels to discover the worst position you can place the pieces in.

3. KNOW YOUR COLOUR

Identifying the patterns and being able to move confidently between them is a major step towards mastering Eye. However, because of the asymmetrical nature of the board's colour distribution, it is also vital that you know the positions of your colour. If you do not, you will waste valuable moves and position your pieces in the wrong places. An expert will also study the positions of the other colours. This will help him to know when to block an opponent's build up and how to capture other colours to eliminate his opponents and increase his control of the board.

This chapter reveals the distribution of each of the colours. It advises on the best tactics you can adopt with the player colours and suggests which neutral colours are worth controlling. You would be wise to read up about each colour, because by understanding your opponents' situation and plans you will be able to disrupt them more effectively.

Positioning The Board

Whichever colour you play always ensure you know where its Short Spiral is. Each time you start a game try to place your colour's Short Spiral in a set position relative to your seat at the table. This will help you to remember its position and you can use the Short Spiral as a useful reference point when moving between the patterns.

The following diagrams have all been annotated to the Red Short Spiral. Place your board in front of you so that the Red Short Spiral is in the same position as it appears in diagram 18. Your board will now match all of the diagrams as you change the patterns.

Each of the player colours has five diagrams to illustrate its distribution. The first four show where that colour appears in the patterns. The last one reveals how the colour is spread across the board's base and is a useful reference for working out where a colour's hidden patterns are. Each set of diagrams is followed by a tactical commentary. The non-player colours are covered as a group at the end of the chapter.

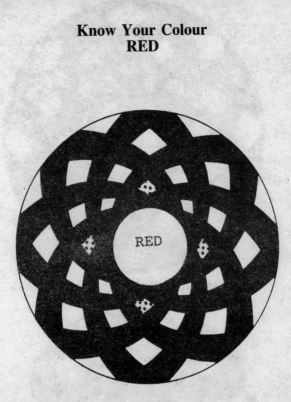

RED

DIAGRAM 17: CIRCLE

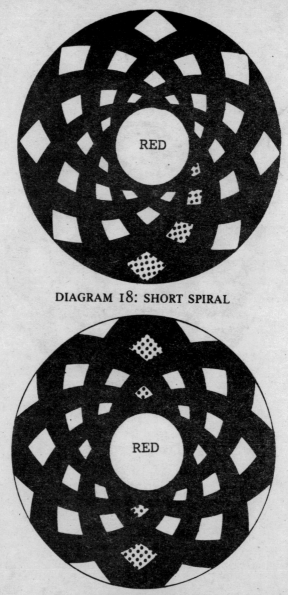

DIAGRAM 18: SHORT SPIRAL

DIAGRAM 19: STRAIGHT

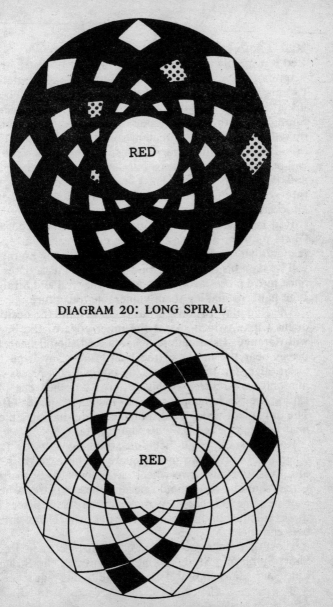

DIAGRAM 20: LONG SPIRAL

DIAGRAM 21: DISTRIBUTION

Red Tactics

Red is probably the easiest colour to play. Its distribution diagram (21) reveals that its squares are concentrated in two main areas of the board. It is obvious Red will be at his strongest if he builds up his pieces around his Short Spiral and on the opposite side of the board. Such a build up will allow Red to threaten capture of both his Short Spiral and Straight Line patterns. At the same time he will be able to cover at least one square of his Long Spiral and two of his Circle. This ability is important in the three- and four-player games if Red is to avoid being knocked out.

Red can play for his Short Spiral, Straight Line and Circle patterns with ease because they are all on top of one another. However, if he plays for his Long Spiral he will weaken his overall position. To control its squares he must move pieces away from his Short Spiral and Straight Line patterns making them vulnerable to capture.

The Red player should always bear in mind the position of his Circle, which shares the inner edge of the board with Orange. Its situation suggests Red should keep his pieces near the inside of the board and away from the outer edge. On the inside of the board Red's pieces can not only cover three of his patterns but they can also exploit the blocking opportunities the inner squares offer. The only place where Red should consider having a piece near the outer edge is by his Short Spiral.

Red possesses four sets of adjoining squares (see diagram 21). The two inner squares of his Straight Line link, with the same two wheel movements, to two of his Circle squares. Red should occupy these squares whenever possible because they are so strong. Place pieces on these squares and get used to the wheel movement between them.

The other links are weaker and exist between Red's Short Spiral and Straight Line patterns and the Straight Line and Long Spiral (see the adjoining squares on diagram 21). All of these links suggest the Straight Line is Red's strongest pattern.

BLUE

DIAGRAM 22: CIRCLE

DIAGRAM 23: SHORT SPIRAL

DIAGRAM 24: STRAIGHT LINE

BLUE

DIAGRAM 25: LONG SPIRAL

DIAGRAM 26: DISTRIBUTION

Blue Tactics

Blue's squares are spread out across the board with an emphasis toward the left-hand side.

The best patterns for Blue to build for are his Circle and Straight Line. The two outer squares of his Straight Line link, with the same two wheel movements, directly to two of his Circle squares. Blue should occupy these squares whenever possible because of the cover they offer and the speed with which they allow him to switch between the patterns. Place some pieces on these squares and get used to the movement between them.

You will recall Red also benefits from this link. However, Red needs to turn the wheels in the opposite direction to enjoy the benefit. Therefore, if each player occupies his strong squares, the first one to move the wheels and use his advantage, will automatically weaken the other player. This is because he will still hold two squares of his colour and be only two moves from the original pattern. Meanwhile, the other player will now occupy two squares of a neutral colour and be two moves away from his strong position. Experiment with the two colours and see for yourself. This situation suggests some careful thought by whichever player moves second. If his opponent builds up on his strong squares he should perhaps consider occupying only one of his own squares and placing a second piece to one side of the other, so it will be moved onto the strong square by his opponent's move. This sort of covering tactic is a clever way to turn an opponent's future move to your own advantage.

Blue also possesses two other sets of adjoining squares (see diagram 26). These link his Straight Line and Short Spiral and his Straight Line and Long Spiral. All of these links suggest, like Red, Blue's strongest pattern is his Straight Line.

Blue's Circle is positioned in the middle of the board (see diagram 22). Pieces positioned in the middle of the board enjoy a greater degree of potential movement than those on the inner or outer edges. Blue can use this advantage over Red to spoil Red's build ups.

The most dangerous pattern for Blue to build for is his Short Spiral. It can be covered from his Circle and Straight Line patterns so should an opportunity arise he can move to capture it. But if the capture takes more than one turn he may find himself too concentrated in one area to protect his other patterns.

Know Your Colour
YELLOW

YELLOW

DIAGRAM 27: CIRCLE

DIAGRAM 28: SHORT SPIRAL

DIAGRAM 29: STRAIGHT LINE

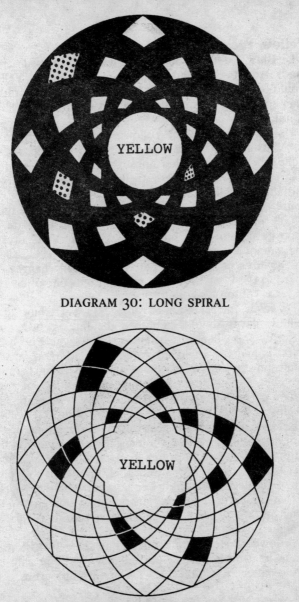

YELLOW

DIAGRAM 30: LONG SPIRAL

YELLOW

DIAGRAM 31: DISTRIBUTION

Yellow Tactics

Like Blue, Yellow's squares are widely dispersed across the board. Its distribution (diagram 31) suggests Yellow would be wise to aim for his Long Spiral or Circle rather than concentrating on capturing a pattern like his Short Spiral.

Unlike Red and Blue, Yellow does not enjoy a strong link between its Circle and Straight Line patterns. All Yellow has is four weaker links of adjoining squares (see diagram 31). Two of these are between his Long Spiral and Circle, while the others are both between his Long Spiral and Straight Line. Annoyingly, in each case these double links are not synchronised because they are on opposite sides of the same wheel's spiral arm. As a result you cannot use them together. If Yellow occupies both link squares in his Circle pattern and then changes the board to the Long Spiral, he will find only one of his two pieces is still on his colour.

However, there is an advantage in everything. The Yellow player should memorise the links between his patterns. This will ensure he always knows where his Long Spiral is and can build up accordingly. Memorising the connecting squares of a colour and then using them as reference points for calculating the position of your hidden patterns is a useful technique every player should employ.

Because all of his links, however incompatible, are to his Long Spiral, Yellow should generally build for this pattern. He should also aim to cover his Circle pattern because this compliments his Long Spiral and will keep one of his pieces near enough to his Short Spiral to protect it from capture by another player. Building up around his Long Spiral will also provide Yellow with a link to his Straight Line.

Yellow's Circle is in a commanding central position. It means he can block other players and still be near to his Circle pattern to capture it if the opportunity arises.

Know Your Colour
GREEN

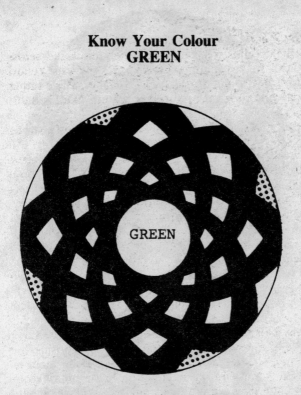

GREEN

DIAGRAM 32: CIRCLE

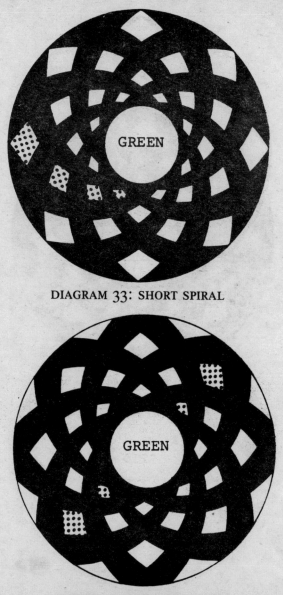

DIAGRAM 33: SHORT SPIRAL

DIAGRAM 34: STRAIGHT LINE

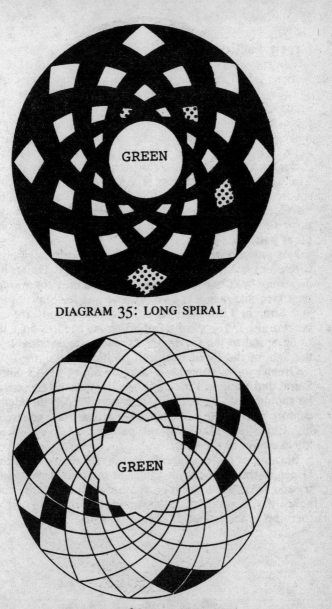

DIAGRAM 35: LONG SPIRAL

DIAGRAM 36: DISTRIBUTION

Green Tactics

Green is probably the hardest colour to win with. This is because its Circle pattern is on the extreme outer edge. The edge restricts the number of positions Green can occupy that will allow one wheel movement to sweep his pieces on to the Circle. In fact there are only two wheel movements to Green's Circle as opposed to the four enjoyed by all the other colours. This limitation makes it easier for other players to block Green's build up for his Circle. A further problem is the distance of the outer squares from the centre of the board. If Green goes for his Circle pattern and fails it will take him at least two turns to get back into a position to capture one of his other patterns.

Not only does Green suffer from a poorly positioned Circle but he also loses out on link squares. Green has no strong links between his patterns and only three weak ones (see diagram 36). Two of these link his Short Spiral and Straight Line patterns but the connections are not synchronised. The third set of adjoining squares links the Long Spiral to the Circle but its value is questionable in the light of the Circle's difficult position.

Green's only strength is the proximity of his Short Spiral and Straight Line patterns. It is around these that he should build up because from here he can threaten a capture whilst being able to cover at least one square of his Circle and Long Spiral patterns to avoid being knocked out of the game.

Because of these handicaps be advised to avoid playing Green in the three-player game. In the four-player game try and fob this colour off on another player! On the other hand, if you want to demonstrate your mastery of Eye then this is the colour to choose.

THE NON-PLAYER COLOURS

The Non-Player Colours

The novice player should concentrate on understanding his own and competing players' colours before he attempts to extend his interest to Orange, Pink, Mauve or Grey.

However, it is important for an expert to be aware of these colours' distribution because they can be used to hinder the build ups of other players. This section will reveal how the non-player colours are spread across the board, what their strengths and weaknesses are and how they influence the player colours.

Know Your Colour: Orange

DIAGRAM 37: ORANGE DISTRIBUTION

Orange is concentrated in two areas of the board in a similar manner to Red. It has three weak links of adjoining squares. Two occur between its Straight Line and Short Spiral patterns but they are not synchronised. The third is between its Straight Line and Long Spiral.

Orange shares the inner ring with Red's Circle pattern, whilst its Short Spiral and Straight Line patterns are sandwiched between Green and Red. As a result these two colours should hold the advantage in being able to capture Orange.

The best tactic in attacking Orange is to go for its Short Spiral or Straight Line patterns. As these are also the tactics for Red and Green these two colours once again hold an in-built advantage for capturing Orange.

Know Your Colour: Pink

DIAGRAM 38: PINK DISTRIBUTION

Pink's squares are widely dispersed making it difficult to capture without risking the loss of your own colour. It possesses only one weak link of adjoining squares between its Long Spiral and Straight Line.

The two player colours which would be least inconvenienced to capture Pink are Blue and Yellow because their pieces should be dispersed across the board when covering their own patterns. Pink's Circle is in the same area as Blue's, whilst its Short Spiral and Straight Lines are sandwiched between Blue and Yellow.

Pink is a powerful colour if you wish to disrupt Red (see p. 68).

Know Your Colour: Mauve

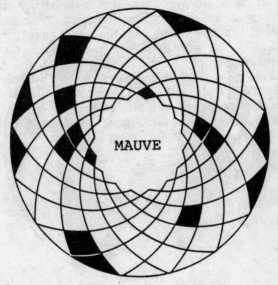

DIAGRAM 39: MAUVE DISTRIBUTION

Mauve's colour dispersion is very favourable, making it one of the easier colours to target and capture. It has five links of adjoining squares between its patterns. Two of these are strong links between its Circle and Straight Line patterns, which are on the outer edge of the board. If some of your pieces get marooned on the outer edge it is worth going for these squares to gain the moves to get the pieces back into the middle of the board. The other three, weaker links are between its Straight Line and Short Spiral, Straight Line and Long Spiral and Circle and Long Spiral.

Mauve's only weakness is that its Circle shares the outer edge of the board with Green and consequently suffers all the disadvantages associated with such a position (see Green tactics p. 58). However, the strong links between its Straight Line and Circle help to compensate for this disadvaantag-

Mauve's Short Spiral and Straight Line patterns are sandwiched between Blue and Green. Green is probably in the best position to capture Mauve. Mauve would be a good choice if you are playing the optional rule of nominating colours for the victory conditions.

Know Your Colour: Grey

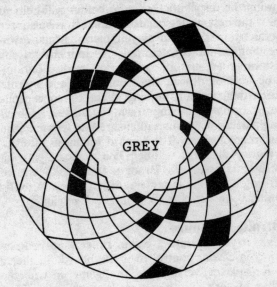

GREY

DIAGRAM 40: GREY DISTRIBUTION

Grey's dispersion is similar to Yellow, whilst it enjoys the strong link squares between its Circle and Straight Line patterns possessed by Blue. Grey also has two sets of unsynchronised links between its Circle and Long Spiral patterns.

Grey's Circle is in the same area of the board as Yellow's, whilst its Short Spiral and Straight Line patterns are found between Yellow and Red. Yellow is in the best position to capture Grey. Grey is a good colour to choose if using the optional rule of nominating colours for the victory conditions.

The best tactic when attacking Grey is to go for its Circle and Straight Line patterns.

Using Your Knowledge Of The Colours

Knowing the distribution of your colour will help you to employ the best strategy in each game. It will also increase the effectiveness of your playing pieces, because you will place them in the correct areas of the board. If you are also aware of your opponents' colour distribution, you will be able to disrupt their build ups and threaten to capture their colour, forcing them to concentrate on defence, instead of trying to win the game.

The pattern diagrams will ensure you form your pieces in the correct areas of the board for each pattern. The distribution diagrams will help you to locate your hidden patterns and assess the strength and weaknesses of the other colours. This last diagram is especially useful for planning your tactics in the Solitaire Eye game.

Controlled Colours

In Eye, if you capture a colour other than your own it will increase your control over the board. In the three- and four-player versions of the game if you capture another player's colour you will knock him out of the game. A word of caution is needed here. Before you eliminate another player, check that none of their pieces are acting as important blocks to stop another of your opponents from winning. If one or more are, only eliminate that player if you can replace the block or win the game before the player who will gain the advantage.

Once you control a colour, at the beginning of each of your turns you can move any other players' pieces that are positioned on it. This can be a good way of breaking up an opponent's formations or removing troublesome blocks. In this light, it is useful to know which of the other colours will most benefit you and which can cause you the most trouble.

No game of Eye will ever be the same because each player will have his own approach. But because players tend to build their pieces up into formations resembling the patterns, a certain degree of uniformity will occur in each game. The analysis below of the relationship between the colours draws its information from the board. It reveals which colours will be occupied by a player if he has built up a formation and is the minimum number of wheel turns away from his target pattern. This is the most likely time when you will be able to react, and therefore it is useful to know which colour you should control to disrupt him the most.

For instance, in diagram 41 blue has positioned his pieces in a Circle formation and is only one clockwise turn of the outer wheel from winning the game. If you set up the board to match this diagram you will find Blue's pieces are occupying the following colours: Orange, Mauve, Pink and Grey. If it was the Red player's turn and he controlled any one of these colours he would be able to break Blue's formation and perhaps even move one of his own pieces in to completely negate it.

DIAGRAM 41: BLUE IN A CIRCLE FORMATION

Each player colour has been analysed in turn according to the above criteria. The overall breakdown for each colour will give you an idea of which colours pose the most threat to that player. The formation charts tell you which colours a player's pieces will occupy if he has built them up for that formation and is about to use the minimum number of wheel turns to reach the desired pattern. To check the information on your own board simply set up that colour's pieces on the desired pattern. Then move the wheels to each of the other board patterns to see where the pieces end up. These new positions will be the ones the charts are recording, because it is from them the player will be able to capture his colour. As you move the pieces you will find that sometimes only three can be moved because a fourth will cause a board block. These blocks have been allowed for on the charts.

The formation charts will tell you which are the best colours to control in order to disrupt an opponent's strategy and formations.

The Threat To Red

Number of positions on the board which are a minimum number of wheel movements from Red's patterns: 92.

The distribution of colours across these squares is as follows:

Orange	12	Red	8
Pink	18	Blue	12
Mauve	12	Green	9
Grey	11	Yellow	10

It is immediately apparent that Pink, if controlled by another player, will cause Red a lot of trouble. Of the player colours, Blue will conflict the most with Red, because in occupying his squares he will reduce the number of positions which are useful to Red.

Red Formation Breakdowns
Short Spiral
22 positions

Orange	2	Red	1
Pink	5	Blue	3
Mauve	3	Green	1
Grey	4	Yellow	3

Main threat: Pink

Circle
24 positions

Orange	4	Red	2
Pink	4	Blue	2
Mauve	4	Green	2
Grey	4	Yellow	2

Straight Line
24 positions

Orange	4	Red	4
Pink	4	Blue	4
Mauve	2	Green	2
Grey	2	Yellow	2

Long Spiral
22 positions

Orange	2	Red	1
Pink	5	Blue	3
Mauve	3	Green	4
Grey	1	Yellow	3

Main threat: Pink

Analysis Of Red Breakdowns
Pink is consistently dangerous for Red and it is a colour that can be most easily captured by Blue.

The Threat To Blue

Number of positions on the board which are a minimum number of wheel movements from Blue's pattern: 92

The distribution of colours across these squares is as follows:

Orange	16	Red	12
Pink	13	Blue	9
Mauve	8	Green	9
Grey	15	Yellow	10

Blue is vulnerable to two neutral colours: Orange and Grey. He will conflict most with the Red player, who is also in the best position to capture Orange.

Blue Formation Breakdowns

Short Spiral
22 positions

Orange	4	Red	3
Pink	3	Blue	1
Mauve	1	Green	1
Grey	6	Yellow	3

Main threat: Grey

Circle
24 positions

Orange	4	Red	2
Pink	4	Blue	2
Mauve	4	Green	2
Grey	4	Yellow	2

Straight Line
24 positions

Orange	4	Red	4
Pink	3	Blue	5

| Mauve | 2 | Green | 2 |
| Grey | 2 | Yellow | 2 |

A good pattern for Blue to build for.

Long Spiral
22 positions

Orange	4	Red	4
Pink	3	Blue	1
Mauve	1	Green	4
Grey	3	Yellow	3

Analysis Of Blue Breakdowns

Orange offers the most consistent threat to Blue's build ups.

Grey stands the greatest chance of disrupting a Blue build up for his Short Spiral.

The Straight pattern is the safest one for Blue to build for.

The Threat To Yellow

Number of positions on the board which are a minimum number of wheel turns from Yellow's patterns: 92.

The distribution of colours across these squares is as follows:

Orange	18	Red	10
Pink	12	Blue	10
Mauve	14	Green	11
Grey	9	Yellow	8

Orange is the danger colour for Yellow. Whilst Green is the player who will conflict most with Yellow's required positioning.

Both Green and Red are in good positions to capture Orange.

Yellow Formation Breakdowns

Short Spiral
22 positions

Orange	5	Red	2
Pink	2	Blue	2
Mauve	5	Green	4
Grey	2	Yellow	0

Main threat: Orange

Circle
24 positions

Orange	4	Red	2
Pink	4	Blue	2
Mauve	4	Green	2
Grey	4	Yellow	2

Straight Line
24 positions

Orange	4	Red	4
Pink	4	Blue	4

72

Mauve	2	Green	2
Grey	2	Yellow	2

Long Spiral
22 positions

Orange	5	Red	2
Pink	2	Blue	2
Mauve	3	Green	3
Grey	1	Yellow	4

Main threat: Orange

Analysis Of Yellow Breakdowns

Orange can be used to disrupt Yellow's build up for both of his spirals.

The lack of yellow squares around his Short Spiral suggests how vulnerable Yellow's overall position will be if he goes for this pattern, as it will be hard for him to cover his other patterns.

The Threat To Green

Number of positions on the board which are a minimum number of wheel turns from Green's patterns: 84.

The distribution of colours across these squares is as follows:

Orange	13	Red	9
Pink	14	Blue	9
Mauve	9	Green	6
Grey	13	Yellow	11

Pink threatens Green as well as Red. Green is also set to conflict with Yellow more than any other player colour.

Green's greatly reduced number of positions is due to the limitations that occur because of its Circle's position on the outer edge of the board.

Green Formation Breakdowns

Short Spiral
22 positions

Orange	3	Red	2
Pink	4	Blue	2
Mauve	3	Green	2
Grey	4	Yellow	2

Circle
16 positions

Orange	3	Red	1
Pink	3	Blue	1
Mauve	3	Green	1
Grey	3	Yellow	1

Straight Line
24 Positions

Orange	4	Red	4
Pink	4	Blue	4

| Mauve | 2 | Green | 2 |
| Grey | 2 | Yellow | 2 |

Long Spiral
22 positions

Orange	3	Red	2
Pink	3	Blue	2
Mauve	1	Green	1
Grey	4	Yellow	6

Main threat: Yellow

Analysis Of Green Breakdowns

Orange and Pink both offer consistent threats to Green.

If Yellow is in the game Green will find it difficult to build up for his Long Spiral.

4. KNOW YOUR PIECES

The third element to mastering Eye is to know how to use your playing pieces. In Eye your playing pieces can both attack and defend. They are attacking whenever you form them into a pattern and threaten to capture a colour. They are defending whenever they are restricting the board's movement, disrupting an opponent's pattern formation, or protecting a colour from capture by occupying one of its squares. On top of this they must also be viewed as a resource, because it is the position of your pieces on the board that will dictate how many moves you have each turn.

You must find a balance between these three functions if you want to win Eye consistently. If you just use them to attack and ignore any defence you will be knocked out of the three- and four-player games very quickly. If you just defend you will not win. If you do not get enough movement points you will get bogged down and start to lose. To add to the problem of finding the right balance, each version of the game gives you only one or two more pieces than you need to capture a colour. You are a commander in charge of limited resources.

It is important you use your pieces correctly as soon as you start to place them. It is at this point you should decide which patterns you are going to play for. You can then start placing your pieces in the correct formation. Your choice of patterns will depend on how the game shapes up but whatever you do always make sure you build up during placement so that you can move easily to more than one pattern. If you limit your choice too much you will come unstuck (see chapter two for advice on which patterns to go for).

At the same time you must keep a wary eye on your opponents. What are they building for? If you do not watch them you may overlook a vital block and lose the game on the first move. I have even seen players lose during placement and before the first move because they have not been watching their opponents.

Another important factor to look out for during placement is the number of moves the player who goes first will have. If you are going first you know that you can dictate how many moves you will have because no one is going to move the board before your turn. Use this advantage. It means you can build up a partial pattern and then use your other pieces to secure the moves you will need to move the board to that pattern, and then complete it with your other pieces. If you are not going first, try to block the leader's formations and create threats that force him to play in positions that are not to his liking.

This chapter covers the tactics of attack, defence and movement.

The Tactics Of Attack

You can use your pieces to attack in a number of direct and indirect ways. When you attack your aim should be to win the game, whilst at the same time tying down your opponents' pieces and obscuring your formations.

To capture a colour through forethought rather than luck you must build up your pieces into formations that match the patterns you are pursuing. Chapter two explains the patterns, whilst chapter three shows you where to build up your colour and which patterns are best to aim for. Unless an opportunity is there for the taking always build for a pattern which is hidden. Sometimes it is worth leaving a formation incomplete but having the final piece only one square away. An incomplete formation attracts less interference from your opponents. Never be afraid to change your formation especially if another player has blocked it.

Make sure you are always in a position to attack. If you are not, you will be losing the game. Try to ensure you always have the following minimum number of pieces attacking.

Game Version	Minimum number attacking
Two Players	3
Three Players	2
Four Players	1

The minimum number is always one less than you need to capture a colour. Such a formation is enough to tie down an opponent's approach piece in defence. At the same time it can be positioned near one of your own defenders and on the turn you change the board he can be slipped in to complete the capture.

To use this tactic you must ensure you have enough movement points to complete the capture. If you use it to capture your own colour it is safe. When you use it to capture a neutral colour or another player's colour more care is needed.

In such circumstances you must first consider the position of the defending piece. Will its movement free an opponent's colour or a neutral colour which is dangerous to you, (see chapter three) for capture? If it does, has your opponent got enough moves to exploit this? If the answer is no to either of these questions make your move. If it is yes, then think again. Are you going to capture the threatening player's colour? If you are and he will be knocked out of the game proceed without fear. If you are not, does he move immediately after you or is there another player who moves first and could fill the gap you are creating? If there is another player who can cover and more importantly will feel obliged to do so, then make your move. This last tactic is called 'passing the buck'.

Passing the buck is a good tactic to employ as long as the other players have no choice but to cover the gap you have created because otherwise they will lose. It is good because it ties down other players' pieces (whilst freeing one of yours) and wastes their movement points.

In the three- and four-player versions of Eye pass the

buck whenever you can, starting with the placement phase. In these versions you have so few pieces you cannot afford to have too many tied up in blocking positions.

The Tactics Of Defence

You must pay attention to your opponents' moves and build ups otherwise you will lose the game. If another player threatens to capture a colour, especially if it is yours, block him as soon as you can. (Unless some other kind soul can be made to do the job for you!)

There are three types of defence in Eye: Pattern Blocks, Board Blocks and Colour Control.

Pattern Blocks

This is the most effective defensive move. When an opponent starts forming his pieces into a pattern, place or move one of your pieces into the formation. The result will be that if he moves the wheels to the desired pattern your piece will occupy one of the colour's squares and block the capture. The only way the player can negate your block is to change his formation. Another possibility occurs if he has control of a colour and can manoeuvre your piece onto it. Then at the beginning of his next turn, if you have not moved the board in the meanwhile, he can move your blocking piece. Keep an eye out for this.

Board Blocks

There are eight positions on the inner edge of the board and eight on the outer edge which if occupied will restrict the movement of the wheels. The inner squares are only available when the board is in its closed position (diagram 42). They stop the inner wheel from turning in an anti-clockwise direction and the outer wheel from turning in a clockwise direction.

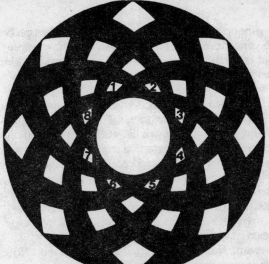

DIAGRAM 42: THE CLOSED EYE AND IT'S EIGHT BLOCKING POSITIONS

DIAGRAM 43: THE OPEN EYE AND IT'S EIGHT BLOCKING POSITIONS

The outer squares are only available when the board is in its open position (diagram 43). They stop the inner wheel from turning in a clockwise direction and the outer wheel from turning in an anti-clockwise direction.

These blocks are not as effective as pattern blocks. They do not negate the power of an opponent's formation and it is still possible to move between all of the patterns. If you move both wheels in the same direction simultaneously they will avoid the effect of such a block. However, they can be used to hold a player up temporarily by stopping him from moving in the one direction he wants to.

Practise with your board and pieces to learn all the effects of these blocks so you can use them effectively in the game. Also look for other players occupying blocking squares. If they do, make sure you build up a formation that needs to turn in one of the free directions.

Colour Control

If you control a colour, at the beginning of each of your turns you may move any opponents' pieces which are occupying squares of that colour. This rule can be used to break up an opponent's formation or remove blocks to your own formations. Chapter three contains a detailed analysis of which are the best colours to control.

The problem with this defence is knowing where to place your opponent's piece so it will not help him. As a general guideline make sure you do not place it in, or near, one of his formations (unless it is already blocked). Try to place it in an area which will least help him. Study the distribution diagrams in chapter three to work out where these areas are. If you can, place it where it will block another player.

Whilst blocking is important it can also tie down too many of your pieces, or force them into positions where they are of no value to you.

To avoid getting too bogged down always follow these ground rules.

If you can pass the responsibility to another player, do so.

If you can see you can win the game before the player you are considering blocking, or you can knock him out before his next turn, do not bother to block him. This will attract attention to him and increase the likelihood no one will notice your winning move.

If you have a choice of blocking positions choose the one that is most advantageous for your colour. Such positions will be near one of your formations or in an area where your colour is concentrated (see chapter three).

Movement

The more moves you have in a turn the quicker you will be able to change formation and you will be better able to foil your opponents' plans.

When building formations always work out how many moves you will need to get to the desired pattern and complete your capture. Then make sure you get the moves.

If you are going first after placement never forget that you can guarantee the number of moves you will get because no one will move the board before your turn.

In the two-player game, if a player completes a formation he will eventually get four moves or win the game. Such formations should be broken up immediately. Use the board blocks to restrict its movement and attack on a different pattern to the player's formation to force him into a defensive game.

In the three- and four-player games it is occasionally worth holding onto a blocked formation just to get the maximum number of moves on your turn.

5. EYE PROBLEMS

Now you know all about Eye it is time to put your knowledge to the test. So here are some problems to solve which will require you to draw on the points made in this book.

Each problem has its own diagram. The diagram shows what pattern your board should be set on. The named colour in the middle of the diagrams tells you the colour of the diagram's shaded squares. Match your board to the diagram so that the coloured squares given are in the correct position.

The playing pieces are represented as follows:

Red playing piece   O
Blue playing piece   ●
Yellow playing piece   ◆
Green playing piece   ⊗

Place the relevant coloured playing pieces on your board according to the diagram's instructions. Then solve the problem.

Feel free to consult the book on any questions the problem may raise. Then work out your answer and compare it to the best answer given at the end of this chapter.

Good luck!

THE PROBLEMS

PROBLEM 1
A Question Of Placement

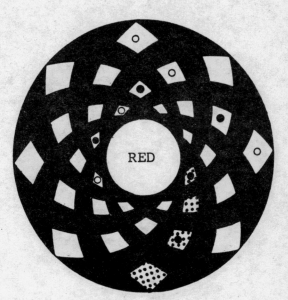

Situation: Two-Player Game.

Order of Play: Red, Blue.

Positon: Both Red and Blue have one more piece to place. It is Red's turn. Where is the best square he could place his piece?

Presuming Red made the best placement, what could Blue do with his last piece to counter Red's position?

PROBLEM 2
Blue's Dilemma

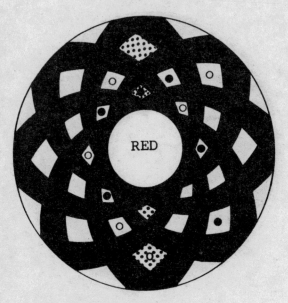

Situation: Two-Player Game
Order of Play: Blue, Red.
It is Blue's turn and he has two moves. What does he
need to do with one of them?

PROBLEM 3
Red Alert?

Situation: Three-Player Game
Order of Play: Blue, Yellow, Red.
Position: It is Blue's move. What is the best result he can get with his three moves?

PROBLEM 4
Out Of The Frying Pan And Into The Fire?

Situation: Three-Player Game
Order of Play: Blue, Red, Green.
Position: It is Blue's turn and he has one move.
Studying the board he sees that Red can win on his next
move by capturing his Long Spiral. With his one move
Blue cannot move a piece to block Red's Long Spiral.
What is his best move to stop Red?

THE ANSWERS

Answer To Problem 1
A Question Of Placement

Red should place his piece on the last remaining Pink square to gain three moves on his turn (remember Red will be moving first).

With his three movement points Red can turn both wheels one step anti-clockwise (if he does this simultaneously none of the inner board blocks will work) and then move a piece to complete his capture of his Long Spiral. This way Red wins the game.

Blue can block Reds winning play by placing his piece on his own Short Spiral next to the piece he already has there. If Red now moves the board as he had planned Blue's piece will be swept onto Red's Long Spiral blocking its capture.

Answer To Problem 2
Blue's Dilemma

An analysis of the situation will tell you Red is in a winning position. On his turn he can move the inner wheel one step clockwise, then move a piece to complete his cature of the Red Long Spiral.

To stop this Blue needs to move his piece on the outer Yellow square to the adjacent outer Pink square. This will then act as a board block stopping Red from turning the inner wheel in a clockwise direction. Blue's second move is open. However, he should not move his pieces on Green or Blue. The piece on Green is covering Red's Long Spiral as well as blocking Red's capture of Green. The piece on the Blue Square is protecting his colour from capture. If Blue used his last move to turn the inner wheel once anti-clockwise, Red could capture Orange, so this move is also to be avoided.

Answer To Problem 3
Red Dilemma?

Blue can win the game. He moves both wheels one step clockwise and then moves a piece to complete his capture of the Blue Circle.

Answer to Problem 4
Out Of The Frying Pan And Into The Fire?

Blue's only hope is to move one of the wheels. Because of the inner board blocks he can only turn the inner wheel once clockwise or the outer wheel once anti-clockwise.

If he turns the inner wheel he will allow Red to capture Pink.

If he turns the outer wheel he will allow Red to capture Yellow.

Blue's best move is to turn the outer wheel. Yellow is far less threatening to Blue than Pink (see chapter three) and in capturing Yellow, Red will break up his Long Spiral formation.